Vena Aguillard:
Woman of Faith

MARSHA BARRETT
Illustrated by John Ham

BROADMAN PRESS
Nashville, Tennessee

© Copyright 1983 • Broadman Press.

All rights reserved.

4242-81

ISBN: 0-8054-4281-2

Dewey Decimal Classification: J266.092

Subject Headings: AGUILLARD, VENA / / MISSIONS—LOUISIANA

Library of Congress Catalog Card Number: 82-73664

Printed in the United States of America

This book is dedicated
with deep appreciation
to
Euna Aguillard Miller,
Maurice Aguillard,
and
Bonnye Miller Reeves
for their willingness
to share with me
their precious memories of
Vena Aguillard.

Contents

Apples for Christmas

Vena Aguillard [ah-gee-ar] looked around at the other students in the school yard. She put her finger to her lips and shook her head slightly as she looked into the face of her younger sister, Euna. Vena did not know who might be listening. She wanted to be sure they were a safe distance away from the school before they began talking. The two girls walked in silence to the edge of the pasture that made up the grounds around their frame school building. Once they were on the road, Euna spoke in rapid French.

"Vena, the teacher said something about extra time off from school. Do you know why?" asked Euna.

"My teacher talked about that, too. But she was talking in English. I couldn't understand all she said," replied Vena. "I think the days off from school have something to do with a holiday."

The girls walked the five miles from the town of Chataignier [sha-TAN-ya], Louisiana, to the small farm where they lived. Eight-year-old Vena and six-year-old Euna chattered away as they walked. They were so glad to be able to talk French without having to watch for the guards who patrolled the school yard. In the early 1900's, students were allowed to speak only English in the schools of South Louisiana. Those who were caught speaking French were reported to the school officials. Vena and Euna knew very little English. They spoke only when they had to while at school. How they looked forward to the end of the school day when they no longer had to be careful about what they said!

"Mom, what holiday is coming soon?" asked Euna when the two girls reached home.

"My teacher said we had some extra time off from school. I think it is because of a holiday," added Vena.

7

"We will talk about things like that later. Right now you need to change your clothes. Your chores are waiting. And your father has some extra things he wants you to do today. Hurry now," said Mrs. Aguillard.

Vena and Euna wasted no time in getting changed and beginning their chores. For the moment, thoughts of school holidays were forgotten. The girls knew their father was waiting, and they did not want to displease him.

Soon Vena and Euna were busy cleaning out the barn. Suddenly, Euna stopped and listened for a moment.

"Do you hear something that sounds like music?" Euna asked. Vena stood still and listened. From far down the road, she could hear the sound of a happy song.

"Oh, Euna! It's Ti Car [tee kar]! And he is singing his Christmas song. That's the holiday that is coming. And that is why we have extra time off from school," Vena said excitedly.

Vena and Euna waved at Ti Car as he came to their front door to talk to Mrs. Aguillard. Ti Car was a harmless old man from Chataignier. Every year, near Christmas, he came by, hoping for some treat. The children were always excited when they heard Ti Car coming down the road, for they knew Christmas was not far off. Chores seemed to go quickly that day as the girls thought about the treats that Christmas would bring.

The sky was still dark several mornings later, but the children in the Aguillard house were already awake. Vena and Euna dressed quickly in the early morning cold. They helped little Otis, their younger brother, who was struggling to get his clothes on. Maurice, an older brother, had already gone to the kitchen. The three younger children soon followed.

Mr. and Mrs. Aguillard were standing by the kitchen table when the children came in. The children stopped and stood motionless. Their eyes sparkled with excitement.

"*Joyeux Noel!* [JWAY-eh No-el] (Merry Christmas!)" said Mr. and Mrs. Aguillard. Then they moved aside. On the table sat shiny red apples, one for each child.

"Apples!" the children shouted with delight. Already their mouths watered as they thought of how good those apples would taste.

8

"I haven't had an apple in two years," said Vena.

"Last Christmas we had oranges. They were good, too," said Euna.

"I don't remember. Have I ever had an apple before?" asked little Otis.

Everyone laughed as they sat down for breakfast. After breakfast, the children hurried to feed the animals and do their morning chores. This was a special day, and they wanted to be ready. Their older brothers and sisters and their families would be here. Friends would probably drop by to visit.

And Christmas dinner! What a treat was in store. Mr. Aguillard had killed a hog. He salted and dried most of the meat for use in the months ahead. But he saved out a fresh pork roast for their Christmas dinner.

"I can already smell the roast," said Vena as the girls returned to the house from their chores.

"It's too early for you to be smelling it. Dinner isn't for a long time, yet," said Euna.

"I know I can't really smell it. But I can already imagine how it is going to smell. And I think I can already taste it, too," laughed Vena, as the girls opened the door and went into the kitchen. They found Mrs. Aguillard busy with bowls and flour. Little Otis looked up and grinned, his face blotched with flour.

"Doughnuts!" both girls said at once. "Can we help, too?"

"There is plenty for everyone to do. Go wash up, and I'll show you how you can help," said Mrs. Aguillard.

Later, as the children looked over the huge platter of doughnuts that awaited family and guests, Mr. Aguillard came into the kitchen.

"Fannie, you must have used every bit of the flour I bought you," Mr. Aguillard told his wife. "That's all the flour you will have until I sell the cotton next fall."

"No, Paul, I didn't use all of the flour," Mrs. Aguillard replied gently. "But today is a special day, and it deserves a special treat."

As Vena helped her mother clean the kitchen, she said, "Mom, I like the blue flowers on that flour sack. I would like to make a dress from it. And I still have the sack you gave me from the last flour Pop bought. I can use it to make a dress for Euna. I'll begin

10

working on them next Sunday, since we won't have school or farm work to do. Oh, and do you have some rags I can use?"

"I don't mind if you use the sack, Vena," said Mrs. Aguillard. "But I'll have to see if I can find some rags. Why do you need the rags, anyway?"

"That's kind of a secret," Vena answered, smiling.

The next Sunday afternoon, the family gathered for their usual Sunday visit. The children played while the grown-ups talked together. But when Mr. Aguillard began to tell some of his wonderful stories, the children stopped their play. They came closer to hear every word. Suddenly, Mrs. Aguillard realized someone was missing.

"Where is Vena?" she asked.

"She has worked on our dresses all day," said Euna. "She finished mine, and it is really pretty. I told her Pop was getting ready to tell stories. I knew she wouldn't want to miss that. But she said she would be here in a little while. She had something she wanted to finish. She wouldn't tell me what it was," Euna finished breathlessly.

Later, when Vena slipped in to join the rest of the family, Mrs. Aguillard asked, "What were you doing that was so important? You missed hearing a story."

"Well, do you remember when I asked you for some rags the other day?" began Vena. "I wanted them so I could make a new doll for Euna. The last time we played with our dolls, I noticed that hers was coming apart."

"A new doll for me?" asked Euna with her eyes dancing. "Oh, Vena! May I see it now?"

Vena left for a moment. When she came back, she held in one hand the pretty new dress she had made for Euna from the printed flour sack. From behind her back, Vena took a new rag doll. The little doll was wearing a pretty new dress just like Euna's.

"Oh, Vena! This is as good a surprise as the apple I got for Christmas!" squealed Euna.

A Boy Named Teddy

"Only two more days until the Sunday night dance," said fifteen-year-old Euna. She was hoeing a field beside seventeen-year-old Vena.

"Maybe just one more day, if someone has a dance party on Saturday night," said Vena, hopefully. "Then I would get to see Teddy twice this weekend," she added, blushing as she said this.

"All you think about is Teddy," giggled Euna. "Maybe he won't be at this dance," she teased.

"Oh, he will be. He has been to every dance I've been to this year. This time he has asked if he can come by and walk me to the dance," said Vena.

"Shall we wear our yellow dresses?" asked Euna. The girls always dressed alike for the weekly dances at the dance hall. They never failed to make an impression on the young men who paid to come in to the dances.

"I don't think Teddy likes me in the yellow dress. Let's wear our pink muslin dresses instead," said Vena.

"Teddy again!" said Euna in mock annoyance. "You won't do anything unless you think Teddy will approve."

The girls continued to pass the time working in the field by talking about the dance that weekend. The dances were the highlight of the week for Vena, Euna, and their friends. As they worked on the farm all week, thoughts of the weekend fun made the hard tasks seem easier.

The next day, just before noon, Vena heard someone coming down the road on horseback. She had been listening for that sound all morning. She ran to the window in time to hear the man on horseback call out to the family inside. Vena listened carefully to

his words. As soon as the horseman left, she quickly went to find Euna.

"Euna, there's to be a *fais do-do* [fay-doe-doe], a dance, tonight, and we are invited!" Vena said excitedly.

Vena was not really surprised to be invited to the dance at a friend's home. She and Euna were good dancers. They were popular with boys and girls alike. They were always included when someone hosted a Saturday night dance in a home. Vena was excited because the occasion gave her extra time to spend with Teddy. Blue-eyed, blond, and handsome, Teddy was sure to be included on the invitation list.

Sure enough, when the time came to leave for the party that evening, Teddy, who lived on the next farm, came to walk with Vena. Euna walked behind with Mrs. Aguillard, who always went along to chaperon her girls. Vena was glad that the party was several miles from her farm. The farther they had to walk, the more time she and Teddy would have together.

What fun the girls had at the party! Vena and Euna were petite and pretty. And because they were such good dancers, they were in demand on the dance floor. Much too soon, midnight came. The partygoers began to depart for home. Once again, Teddy found his way to Vena's side.

"May I walk you home?" he asked.

"I would like that. Let me ask Mom," said Vena. Vena found her mother where she had been sitting throughout the dance.

"Mom," she began, "Teddy wants to walk home with me. Is that all right with you?"

"I don't mind, Vena. But remember, I will be walking behind you. Stay close enough for me to see you in the lantern light," Mrs. Aguillard reminded Vena.

Vena smiled her thanks at her mother as she moved away to find Teddy again.

Teddy continued to walk Vena to and from the dances each weekend. Often, he would come to the Aguillard home to visit with Vena. Vena and Teddy's friendship grew. One day, Teddy came to talk to Mr. Aguillard about something very important.

"Sir," Teddy began, "I love your daughter, Vena. I would like your permission to ask her to be my wife."

14

Mr. Aguillard happily gave his consent. After all, Teddy's family was considered wealthy compared to the Aguillards. Mr. Aguillard knew Teddy was a good "catch" for a girl from a poor family.

Later, Vena came in the house after visiting with Teddy on the porch of the Aguillard home. Her eyes were shining as she showed her family the ring and gold necklace Teddy gave her to seal the promise of their engagement.

The next two years were full of preparations for the upcoming marriage. Vena filled her hope chest with lovely things for her future life with Teddy. One day, Vena told her family some exciting news.

"Teddy and I have found the perfect house for our first home. We are going to collect furniture to go in it right away," Vena said.

To Vena, it seemed that everything in her life was perfect. She was wrapped in a cloud of happiness as she and Teddy planned toward their wedding day.

"Surely, nothing could make me happier than I am right now," Vena thought dreamily to herself.

Little did Vena know that events lay just ahead that would change the way she thought about everything.

The Decision

Knock! Knock! A man stood at the front door of the Aguillard home.

"Hello. My name is Dolzey McGee," the young man said, as Mrs. Aguillard answered the door. "May I come in and read to you from the Bible?" he asked.

Mrs. Aguillard hesitated for a moment. Although her family seldom went to church, they considered themselves a part of the traditional religion of the French-speaking people of Louisiana. But no one had ever asked to read the Bible to her before. In fact, their local priest taught that only a priest could read and interpret the Bible.

"Still, it is God's Word," she thought. "I can't refuse to listen to God's Word. And it would be rude to turn the young man away."

"Yes, come in," Mrs. Aguillard said, at last.

Mr. McGee sat down and began to read the Bible to Mrs. Aguillard. From another room, Vena and Euna heard Mr. McGee reading to their mother.

"I've never heard anything like that," Vena said. "We have always been told that we would not be able to understand the Bible ourselves. But it is wonderful!"

Before Mr. McGee left, he invited the Aguillard family to attend the Baptist church where he was preaching. Vena did not really know why, but she knew she had to hear more from the Bible. In spite of the fact that she had been taught that it was a sin to go to a Protestant church, Vena knew she had to go to that meeting.

Dolzey McGee preached from the fifth chapter of the Book of Daniel. As he talked about the story of the feast of King Belshazzar, words began to pound in Vena's mind. Over and over

17

Vena heard, "worldly friends . . . handwriting on the wall . . . weighed in the balances and found wanting."

"How does that preacher know so much about me?" Vena wondered, astonished. "How did he find out about my dancing and my worldly friends?"

For Vena, a hand wrote that night, "weighed in the balance and found wanting." Suddenly she saw her life wasting away in dance halls.

Vena could not sleep that night or for many nights to follow. Also unable to eat, she soon became ill. Her family did not know of Vena's great inward struggle. But they knew something was making her sick. Mr. and Mrs. Aguillard decided to send Vena to Charity Hospital in New Orleans, Louisiana. There, they hoped doctors would find the cause of Vena's mysterious illness.

Vena spent three weeks in the New Orleans hospital. She was miserable the whole time. But gradually she began to make decisions.

"I can't continue to practice the empty ritual of the religion I've been taught all my life," Vena thought to herself. "And the dances! Why, they have been the most important part of my life, next to Teddy. But they seem so worthless now."

One day, a student from Baptist Bible Institute came into Vena's hospital room. "My name is L. C. Smith," he said, introducing himself. After a short visit, Mr. Smith quoted John 14:6 in French. "Jesus saith unto him, I am the way, the truth, and the life: no man cometh unto the Father, but by me" is the verse Mr. Smith quoted. Then he prayed and left.

Vena was alone to think about what she had heard. "Everything is clearer to me now," she thought. "At least I know what to do. But how do I do it?" Vena wondered.

When Vena became strong enough to return home from the hospital, she found a big change in her family. Everyone in the family had accepted Jesus as Savior. The Aguillard home was transformed!

The most noticeable change was in Mr. Aguillard. Even though he loved his family, he had been a hard man to live with. Cursing and drinking were his regular habits. But now he was a different man. He no longer drank. Even his face was changed. His dark eyes sparkled. And he whistled happily as he went about his work.

Vena made another discovery. Her brother, Maurice, also had accepted Jesus while he was away in the Navy. He came home eager to tell his family what had happened. What a surprise he had when he arrived home! Twenty-two other family members had become Christians, also.

Vena, still struggling with her personal decision, felt suddenly out of place in her own home. When family members shared their new joy with her, that only added to her discomfort. Vena also saw that family friends were not happy about what the family had done. When they learned that the Aguillards had joined the Chataignier Baptist Church, they refused to speak to any of the family. Lifelong friends turned their backs rather than accept the idea of a French Louisiana family leaving the traditional church and religious practices.

One evening, while the family was eating dinner, an older Aguillard son, Dennis, ran into the house.

"Pop! Help me! They're after me! They are going to kill me! They have knives!" Dennis gasped.

"The rest of you go hide in the cotton field," said Mr. Aguillard. "I'll get my gun to help Dennis."

Later, Dennis told the family what had happened. "My brother-in-law and his friends have threatened us since we joined the Baptist church," he said. "They said that they would kill us if we would not go back to our old religion. I don't know if they really would have killed us, but I knew I couldn't wait around to see!"

Vena was having her own problems with her friends. When they learned that the Aguillard family had all become Christians, they did everything to keep Vena from joining the church.

"Oh, I don't know what to do," cried Vena. "My plans for the future, as well as my friends, will be lost if I do accept Jesus as my Savior. But I am miserable like I am. I cannot go on without God," she said.

Teddy resented Vena's interest in Jesus. "You will have to make a choice," he said. "You can have Jesus, or you can have me, but you can't have both." Then Teddy offered Vena everything he had to try and persuade her to forget about God and choose him instead.

19

"Teddy, I don't understand all of this myself," Vena said. "All I know is that I cannot turn back. I must learn more about God, even if I die trying."

Vena knew her plans were worthless if she did not have Jesus as her Savior. She knew she had to make a decision.

The next day, the family sat down for the noon meal. Vena watched as her mother bowed her head to quietly pray. It was the first time Vena had ever seen this. Suddenly she jumped up from the table and ran to her room. She fell on her knees and cried to the Lord to save her.

"What happened next is hard to explain," Vena said later. "I could almost see a heavy weight being lifted off of me. I felt like I was suddenly in another world. Everything around me was more beautiful."

During the next week, Vena carefully put her engagement ring and necklace in a box. She knew she must return them when Teddy came on Saturday. Vena also knew it would be the hardest thing she had ever done.

Much too soon Saturday arrived, and Teddy was at the door. Vena staggered as she crossed the room to him. Slowly, she placed the box in Teddy's hand. Teddy looked at the ring and necklace a long time.

"Please keep the necklace to remember me by," said Teddy. Then he put his head in his hands and began to cry. Teddy was still sobbing a while later when Vena watched him go out into the night and out of her life forever.

Vena turned to go to her room, certain that she, too, would cry herself to sleep that night. Instead, Vena felt the Lord's presence surround her in that room. She knew right then that no matter what she gave up, the Lord would have something better for her in return.

Vena was ready to make a public statement of her faith in Jesus. She wanted to be baptized and join the church. But Vena was still too weak to go to church. One day twelve members of the Chataignier Baptist Church came to Vena's home.

"You do not have to wait until you are strong enough to come to the church building," they told her. "The people are the church.

20

You can join the church right now. Later, when you are stronger, you can be baptized."

"Oh, thank you," Vena said. "I've struggled so long to make the decision to accept Jesus as my Savior. Now that I have done it, I want to go ahead and become a church member also."

Before the church members left, they collected an offering among themselves. They gave the offering to Vena, saying, "We want to give you something to let you know of our love and encouragement. We will see you in church as soon as you are stronger."

A Taste of Missions

"I think you should go away for awhile, Vena," said Mrs. Aguillard. "You still aren't strong. And you need to be away from the people who are saying such terrible things about our family. I'm sure a rest will do you good. Your aunt spent some time in Cameron, Louisiana. She thinks the sea air will be good for you. Pop will take you to Cameron next week."

The following week, Mr. Aguillard drove Vena to Lake Charles, Louisiana. From there, they went by boat to Cameron. Mr. Aguillard stayed a few days to get Vena settled in a boardinghouse. But soon he had to return home. Vena was alone in a strange place.

The people at the boardinghouse were very curious about Vena. They asked all kinds of questions.

"What are you doing here?"

"Do you have a family?"

"Why is a pretty girl like you sitting here alone? You should be out having fun with other young people."

Vena welcomed the questions. Each question gave her a chance to tell what had happened in her life. Vena was so glad to tell others about the difference since Jesus came into her life to be her Savior.

Mr. and Mrs. Peshoff, who ran the boardinghouse, especially liked Vena. They were pleased when Vena became friends with their daughter, Larmie. What fun those two girls had together! Vena taught Larmie every hymn she knew. Then the two girls spent hours singing praises to Jesus. The Peshoff family had not heard about Jesus before. But they listened to Vena. And they watched her as she lived with them that summer. Eventually, each member of the family became a Christian. Many years later, two of Larmie's children became missionaries.

That summer in Cameron was an important one in Vena's life. For the first time since becoming a Christian, she shared her new faith with others.

"I believe this is what I am supposed to do," thought Vena. "I believe the Lord wants me to spend my life telling others about Jesus." Excitement began to rise within Vena as she thought about sharing Jesus with people everywhere.

Vena knew that if she were going to tell others about Jesus, she needed to learn more about the Bible. She enrolled in Acadia Baptist Academy in Eunice, Louisiana. Vena had not attended school since the fifth grade, so studying at the academy was a whole new experience. But Vena was excited about the people she met and the things she discovered at the academy.

"When I became a Christian, few people back home believed as I did," Vena said to a fellow student. "What a surprise I found when I came here. Why, Baptists have mission work all over the world! And so many people want to tell others about Jesus, just as I do."

Vena became an enthusiastic member of the Mission Band at the academy. She loved going out to the surrounding towns to tell others about Jesus. More and more, Vena began to realize that this was what the Lord wanted her to do. Then one day, she received an invitation to do something else.

"Vena, you know the academy needs money," said a school official. "You have such an interesting story to tell about how you became a Christian. We would like for you to go out with some of the other students to represent the academy. As you speak to groups, we hope the people will give money to help support the school," he said.

Vena began to travel to many towns and communities. She told how she became a Christian. She told the people why she came to Acadia Baptist Academy to study. As Vena spoke, the people understood how important it was to help the academy. They gave money so the school could continue to teach and train young people to serve God.

As Vena spent more time traveling to speak about the academy,

she had less time to work with the Mission Band. Vena was glad to help her school. But she missed meeting people and telling them about Jesus. She talked to God about the way she felt.

"Lord, I'm glad you can use me to help the academy," Vena prayed. "But I miss talking to people about Jesus. Please, Lord, let me do some kind of mission work while I am out of school for the summer. Whatever you lead me to do, I know it will be the right place for me. Amen."

Not long after that, Vena received an invitation from a lady named Mary Lou Jenkins. "I will pay your room and board if you will spend your summer in Abbeville, Louisiana," the invitation began. "While you are here, I want you to tell the French-speaking people about Jesus."

"Thank you, Lord, for hearing and answering my prayer," said Vena, as she prepared to go to Abbeville.

A Postcard Full of Promises

"I don't think you will have much success reaching people for Jesus here," said A. D. Maddry, pastor of the small English-speaking church in Abbeville. He and his wife offered to help Vena in any way they could. But they knew how hard it was to break through superstition and prejudice.

Vena did not know where to begin. She knew that somehow she would have to find people who would listen to the Bible. But she also knew that she still did not know much about the Bible herself. Above all, Vena knew that if anything were going to be done in Abbeville, the Lord would have to do it.

For three days, Vena stayed in her room alone. She went through the Bible looking for Scriptures that said God would answer prayer. Vena wrote the promises on a postcard and placed it in her Bible. Then she committed herself and the people of Abbeville to the Lord in prayer. She asked the Lord to open up a way for her to share the good news about Jesus with others.

Believing that the Lord would answer her prayer, Vena started out. She walked the streets of Abbeville looking for anyone who would listen to the Bible. After a while, Vena saw a woman washing her clothes in the yard.

"Hello," Vena said, approaching the woman. "May I read something wonderful to you?" she asked.

The woman agreed to listen. As Vena read, the woman listened with growing interest.

"Would you go with me to my sister's house? I want her to hear what you read to me," the woman said.

Vena went with the woman to the home of her sister, Mrs. LeBlanc. The three women sat down under a tree. Vena began to

read to them from God's Word. The women listened intently, a look of wonder on their faces.

"Would you share with my husband what you just read to us?" asked Mrs. LeBlanc. "He is working over in that field."

Mr. LeBlanc refused to listen. But as Vena left, she said to him, "I'll be praying for you."

Walking back across the field with the two ladies, Vena told them about an idea she had.

"I want to find a place where I can invite several people at once to come together and hear the Bible," Vena said. "If I keep on reading the Bible to just one person at a time, I won't be able to reach many people in a summer."

"We know someone who might help," said the two sisters. "A lady we know might let you meet in her house." Vena and the two sisters went to see the woman.

"Yes, you may use my living room for a meeting," the woman said. "Why don't you meet here on Tuesday evenings?" she suggested.

Vena prayed about the Tuesday night meeting for the rest of the week. Everywhere she went, she invited people to come. But she was not prepared for what happened on Tuesday night.

When Vena opened the door to go in for the first meeting, she could hardly believe her eyes. Forty-five people were crowded into that living room, waiting to hear from God's Word! Vena looked around at the faces of the people. Suddenly, she saw someone she knew. Mr. LeBlanc, the man who had refused to listen to the Bible, sat at the very back of the crowded living room. Vena knew for sure that God was at work in Abbeville.

The Tuesday night meetings continued for the rest of the summer. Vena still visited as many people as she could during the week. By the end of the summer, she had read the Bible to 440 people.

Summer was quickly coming to an end. Vena wanted to reach as many people as possible before she returned to school. She remembered that L. C. Smith had visited her when she was in the New Orleans hospital. She thought about how he shared God's Word and prayed for her. Vena invited Brother Smith to come and

28

preach in Abbeville. When he came, he brought something with him.

"A tent!" exclaimed Vena, when she saw what he had. "What a perfect place to have the meetings. Most people would never go inside a Protestant church. But I think they will come to a tent meeting," she said excitedly.

The very first night of the meeting, a wonderful thing happened. Mr. and Mrs. LeBlanc and their three daughters all accepted Jesus as their Savior. Before the summer ended, one hundred people became Christians. The little English-speaking church began a French-speaking Sunday School.

As Vena prepared to go back to the academy, she thought back over the summer in Abbeville. "Nothing is impossible with God," she thought to herself.

Returning to Acadia Academy, Vena participated in the Mission Band and the speaking trips as she had before. But something was wrong. The mission work no longer seemed effective. Four students, including Vena, met together to decide what to do.

"We are going out to share with others, but we are not spending enough time in personal prayer and Bible study," they said. The four students decided to meet every day. They asked a professor to meet with them. Each day, they prayed for themselves and for the school. The professor led them in Bible study. The more the students learned about God, the more boldly they prayed. They began to see that God did what the Bible said he would do. The students began to feel that the Lord was going to do something exciting in their school.

Four months after the students began meeting, a preacher named Herschel Stagg came to the academy to preach a week-long revival.

"Now we will see God answer the prayers we have prayed for our school," Vena thought, as she went to the first revival meeting. But at the close of the service, only one boy accepted Jesus as Savior.

How disappointed Vena felt as she returned to her room that night! For awhile, she tried to study. But her disappointment crowded in to distract her thoughts. Unable to concentrate, Vena decided to visit Brother Stagg.

What a surprise awaited Vena when she arrived at Brother Stagg's door! Students were already waiting in a long line to visit with the preacher. Vena went back to her room and found another surprise. The room was full of girls praying. And as Vena looked out the window, she saw groups of boys praying in the moonlight.

The rest of the week was a busy one as the Lord worked in people's lives. Money and other items were returned to their rightful owners. Students asked forgiveness of one another for things they had said and done.

"Now I see what has been wrong with our mission work all year," thought Vena. "Just as leaves and trash can build up and stop water from flowing, wrong actions and attitudes can build up to stop God's power from flowing through people's lives."

By the end of the week, the campus seemed a different place. Many people had a renewed relationship with the Lord. Many accepted Jesus as their Savior.

Vena completed her studies at Acadia Baptist Academy. Looking back on her experiences there, she said, "I have learned so much about the Bible at the academy. But the months of prayer and Bible study, and the revival with Brother Stagg, taught me more about mission work than I could have ever learned in a class."

After leaving the academy, Vena felt that she needed more training. She decided to go to the Baptist Bible Institute in New Orleans, Louisiana. One day a professor asked the students to pray about something.

"I preach every Sunday to a few Christians in Morgan City, Louisiana. But thousands of people there do not know Jesus. Students, please pray that God will send someone to Morgan City. Pray that God will find just the right person to share Jesus' love with those people," pleaded the professor.

Vena began to pray for the people in Morgan City. She longed for them to know about Jesus. "Send someone to share your love with those people," Vena prayed repeatedly.

One day a visitor came to the campus. The visitor, a man named Dr. Lawrence, was from the Home Mission Board of the Southern Baptist Convention. He came to the campus to talk with the students about mission work. One day he talked with Vena.

"Miss Aguillard," began Dr. Lawrence. "We would like you to

go to Morgan City to work with the people there who do not know Jesus as their Savior."

Almost before Dr. Lawrence finished talking, Vena answered. "Yes, I will go. When do I begin?" she replied eagerly. Only later did Vena realize that she did not even find out how much the job would pay!

Vena found that many Christians in Morgan City had the same attitude as those in Abbeville. They had tried everything, but no one would come to hear God's Word. Vena did not let their attitude discourage her. She remembered the postcard full of promises that she had in her Bible. Vena pulled out the card and read the promises. Then she began to pray.

"Lord, I know you sent me to this place," Vena prayed. "And I know that you can make a difference in this town. I trust you to show me what to do next. I thank you that you will open the way to reach these people."

The next day, Vena started out with her Bible under her arm. She hoped to find someone who would let her read the Bible to them. Soon she came to a house with four children in the yard.

"May I come in and read the Bible to you?" Vena asked the mother. But she refused to listen. Vena looked at the four children who did not know about Jesus.

"Would you mind if I tell a story to your children?" Vena asked.

"I guess a story won't hurt anything," the mother answered.

Vena sat down with the children and began to tell a Bible story. The three little girls and the little boy listened with excitement to the wonderful words. All too soon the story came to an end.

"I will tell more stories down at the Hall on Sunday. I'll ask your mother if you can come," Vena told the children.

"You may take the children with you," said the mother, "but you will have to come and get them ready."

Vena was not sure what the mother meant by "getting them ready," but she agreed to do it.

"They don't have the right kind of clothes to wear to church," the mother said. "Here is some material you can use to make them some clothes."

"Oh, my!" thought Vena. "How will I ever do it?" Then she

32

remembered the flour sack dresses she had made long ago for herself and her sister.

"Surely if I could make dresses from flour sacks, I can make something from this nice piece of fabric," thought Vena. On Saturday, Vena took the new clothes to the children's house.

"The children will need haircuts before they go to church," their mother said.

Vena had never cut hair before. But she wanted those children in church. She decided to start by cutting the hair of the three girls.

"Well, they don't look too bad," Vena thought when she finished. "Now to do something about the boy's hair."

Vena worked and worked trying to get his haircut even. First she trimmed one side, then the other.

"I'm glad hair grows back," thought Vena, looking at the finished haircut. "He looks like he has been scalped!"

When Sunday came, Vena showed up at the Hall with four children in odd clothes and strange haircuts. That did not seem like much of a beginning. But God was at work.

The children's mother told her friends that if they needed anything done, Vena Aguillard would do it free. Telephone calls came for Vena to do all kinds of things. She cleaned houses, baby-sat, sewed, cooked, and anything else people asked her to do. Everywhere she worked, Vena made new friends. She told her new friends about the Sunday meetings at the Hall. As the people learned to trust Vena, they began to come to the services.

Before long, the Hall was too small to hold the crowds that came. The Home Mission Board bought a lot so a new church building could be built. The lot was perfect for a new church. But there was one problem. Before building could begin, the lot had to be cleared of weeds. When Vena could find no one to clear it, she decided to do the work herself.

For three weeks, Vena worked with a swing knife. When she finally reached the end of the lot, weeds were growing again at the other end.

"It is urgent that building begin immediately!" Vena wrote to the Home Mission Board. Cleaning that lot once was enough!

Men came to build the new church. Vena then realized that someone needed to supervise the builders. But she could find no one to do it. Vena decided to supervise the work herself. Every day Vena watched the men as they worked. But she was careful not to say much to the men. She did not want them to find out that she knew nothing about building!

By the time the church was complete, the building was already too small for the crowds. The people decided to call a pastor. The church continued to grow. Soon the little church, that began with four children who listened to Bible stories, had to build a still larger building.

"The promises in the Bible are right," thought Vena. "Nothing is impossible with God."

Crisis

"Dear Miss Aguillard," the letter began. "Will you consider coming to Crowley, Louisiana? The First Baptist Church of Crowley just rented a building in West Crowley. We want to begin a mission in that area. We feel like you are the right person to help start the mission."

When Vena arrived in Crowley, she found another "impossible" situation. No one offered her much hope of success in reaching people with the good news of Jesus.

"The situation in Crowley sounds like what I found in Abbeville and Morgan City. If God could work in those places, he can work here," Vena said, as she started out with her Bible.

Day after day, Vena walked the streets. She seemed to get no responses from the people. How alone she felt. Since giving her life to Jesus, Vena had never been so disheartened. She was ready to give up.

One day, when Vena was feeling very discouraged, some friends came through town and stopped to visit her. "Oh, Vena," they said. "You look so tired. You are working much too hard. You need to get away and rest. Why don't you come with us to California? A change will be good for you."

"Maybe that is what I should do," said Vena. "I am not accomplishing anything here. A change probably would be good for me."

Vena packed her belongings and went to California with her friends. Immediately, Vena loved the warm climate and the informality of the people.

"This is where I want to stay," said Vena. "I will find a job. As soon as I can, I will get an apartment of my own."

Vena had no trouble finding a job in a store. At first, she enjoyed

36

the colorful merchandise and the busy shoppers that surrounded her all day long. But soon things began to go wrong.

"Miss, I think you have given me the wrong package," said a customer.

"Vena, those towels don't go there. And I found the buttons you put away mixed in with the stationery. What has happened to your memory?" asked her boss.

"I gave you five dollars. You gave me change back for one dollar," said another customer.

Vena looked down at the money a customer gave her. "Is that a fifty-cent piece and two nickels, or a quarter and two dimes?" she thought. "I can't even tell what the money is anymore. I don't think this is the place for me."

Vena told her boss that she would not be back. She packed her belongings and returned to Crowley.

"I see clearly that God wants me in missions work," Vena said. "No matter how hard the work becomes, he will give me strength to do it. I know now that I can never be happy doing anything else."

God used the time that Vena was in California. She came back to the West Crowley mission with new strength and enthusiasm. Never again did she doubt that God called her to missions work.

Once again, Vena walked the streets and knocked on doors. Gradually, she found people who would listen to God's Word. One year later, the mission in West Crowley had a Sunday School with classes for all ages.

When Vena received frequent invitations to speak in other places, attendance dropped at the mission. The First Baptist Church of Crowley decided the time had come to organize the mission into a church. The newly formed church called its own pastor.

"Oh, Lord," Vena prayed, "I praise you for the hard days when I first came to Crowley. I thank you for allowing me to have the experience in California. I can always look back to that time and know for sure that you have a purpose for me. And now, just look at the new church you have started in West Crowley. Everyone said it could not be done. But nothing is impossible with you."

Three Months That Never Ended

"I wonder who sent this letter from Atlanta," said Vena, opening her mail. She discovered that the letter was from Dr. Courts Redford, Executive Secretary of the Home Mission Board.

"He wants me to come to Atlanta for a conference with him," Vena said. "I think I already know what he wants. He is going to ask me to be a field-worker. Why, that means traveling all over the United States! I get lonely when I leave Louisiana, even for a little while. And if I am speaking in meetings, I won't get to do personal mission work. It will be just like when I spoke for the Acadia Baptist Academy. Besides that, I get sick riding on trains!"

Vena knew she at least had to go talk to Dr. Redford. On the way to Atlanta, Vena wrote a speech. She included all of the reasons why she could not become a field missionary. When Vena arrived in Atlanta, she delivered her speech to Dr. Redford.

Instead of the understanding reaction Vena expected, Dr. Redford seemed not to have even heard her! He calmly began to explain the duties of a field-worker. He obviously still planned for Vena to represent the Home Mission Board as a field missionary.

Vena continued to object to Dr. Redford's plan. But he suggested a compromise.

"Miss Aguillard, will you consider working as a field missionary for a three-months trial period? That way you can find out how the work suits you," Dr. Redford said.

Vena thought for a few moments. Finally, she said, "All right, I will try it for three months only." To herself, Vena thought, "And I know those will be the longest three months of my life."

But something strange happened as Vena began to travel to speak in churches and meetings. She found that she loved sharing

39

about missions with others. She never knew when the three months ended! For twenty-five years, Vena would never completely unpack her suitcase.

What adventures Vena had as she traveled around the country! Often, Vena was invited to speak in schools of missions. During a school of missions, a group of missionaries spent a week in an area. Every day, each missionary spoke in a different church in that area. One such school of missions was in North Carolina.

Vena arrived at the place where she would speak the first night. She found that it was not a church building, but an old tabernacle building. Kerosene lamps gave off a soft light over the congregation. Vena got up and began to speak. She told of her own experiences in missions work. She also told of missions work in other places. As Vena spoke, a hush settled over the people. Then Vena heard shuffling sounds.

"What is happening?" she wondered. Vena tried to tell what was making the noise, but she could see little in the dim lamplight. Vena heard a new sound—the sound of soft crying. Then Vena realized what was happening. The shuffling sounds were made as the people slid from the wooden benches to kneel and pray. Quietly Vena spoke to the people.

"The Holy Spirit is here with us. You don't need me to talk any more. I will leave you now. You continue to pray and let the Lord work," Vena said. Then she slipped out of the tabernacle.

The experience in North Carolina was one which repeated itself over and over again. Vena was a tiny, quiet woman. But when she began to speak to a group, God's mighty power would begin to work in the hearts of the people. Vena's faith in God and in his Word came through every word she spoke.

One time Vena was invited to a church in Kentucky. A winter storm covered everything with a deep blanket of snow and ice. When Vena arrived at the train station, she found that she had a problem.

"I'm sorry, lady," said the ticket agent. "None of the passenger trains are running. Maybe tomorrow, if the tracks are clear, the trains will be running. Check back then."

"But sir, I have to speak in a church tonight!" Vena said.

"I'm sorry. I can't do anything about the snow," said the ticket agent.

"Lord," Vena prayed silently, "If you want me to speak, you will have to get me there."

Just then a man walked over to Vena. "I am the engineer of a freight train. I'll be leaving soon. We pass through the town where you want to go. If you don't mind riding in the caboose, you are welcome to go with us."

How Vena got to her speaking engagements was not important. She cared only about getting there to share the message of Christ.

"I would be delighted to ride in your caboose," replied Vena. The engineer helped her get settled as comfortably as possible. During the long ride, the train men showed Vena where the coal went and how the train worked. They seemed pleased to have Vena riding their caboose. They treated her like an honored guest.

At last, the train arrived. Vena thanked the men who had helped her. She found a phone to call the pastor of the church where she was to speak.

"This is Vena Aguillard," she said over the phone. "I am at the train station."

"But you can't be here!" the surprised pastor said. "No trains are running because of the ice and snow!"

Vena chuckled to herself. She knew that nothing could stop God from getting his message through.

Whether Vena was speaking at a small church to a few people, or to thousands at a meeting of the Southern Baptist Convention, she had one handicap that caused problems for her. She did not look like a missionary. Tiny in size, with dark hair and pretty features, she did not fit the picture that many people had of women missionaries. Sometimes this got Vena into some funny situations.

On one occasion, Vena's train arrived late in Nashville, Tennessee. She was to speak at a state Woman's Missionary Union convention. Breathlessly, Vena arrived at the auditorium. She could hear the large group of women singing inside as she approached the door.

"May I go in, please?" Vena asked the tall, blonde girl at the auditorium door.

"I'm sorry, but you can't go in until after the speaker finishes," the girl firmly replied.

Vena tried to make the girl understand that she *was* the speaker. But with an auditorium full of singing women and Vena's French accent, the girl could not understand.

Gathering all her strength, Vena shouted as loud as she could, "If you don't let me in, there won't be a speaker!" The surprised girl said, "Oh, excuse me! I never would have dreamed you were a missionary."

Vena quickly apologized for yelling. Taking a program, Vena pointed out her name. Then she ran on to the platform just in time to hear herself being introduced.

During World War II, passenger trains often were converted to troop trains to carry soldiers. Of course, the servicemen came first. But if any room remained, other passengers could ride, also. Vena rode such a troop train to a speaking engagement in Oklahoma.

Settling herself in a seat by a window, Vena looked around at the other travelers. "I seem to be the only one not in uniform," Vena said. "Thank you, Lord, for providing a seat for me."

As the train gathered speed, Vena could feel smoke and coal dust coming through the open window. "I can't close the window," Vena thought. "The air would get too stuffy. I'll just have to wash up at the train station before I go to speak."

Vena got as comfortable as possible. She needed to sleep, if she could. She would arrive at her destination just in time to get to the church to speak at the morning worship service.

Sunlight coming through the train window wakened Vena. She shifted in the cramped seat. Soon Vena heard the conductor call her stop.

Vena was the only person who got off the train in the small Oklahoma town. She hurried toward the station to wash up. Then she realized that the building was dark and locked. Looking around, Vena saw no one to meet her. Far down the road, she saw a man coming in a wagon.

"Sir, may I ride into town with you?" Vena asked. "I am to speak this morning at the Baptist Church."

The man looked strangely at Vena. Then he nodded toward the back of the wagon.

43

"I'll take you into town just as soon as I pick up the mail," he said, still staring at Vena.

Sunday School was just over when the wagon pulled up in front of the church. A woman saw Vena sitting in the back of the wagon.

"Can I help you in some way?" the woman asked Vena.

"My name is Vena Aguillard. I am here to speak in your church this morning," Vena replied.

"Lord, have mercy on us!" the woman cried, with a horrified look on her face.

Only then did Vena realize that the smoke and coal dust coming in the train window had turned her face into a black, sooty mess. Getting up to speak, Vena said, "Come back tonight, and I promise you that I will look better by then."

The people did return that evening to hear her speak again. But many never did believe that she was the same woman they saw that morning.

Many times people would say things to Vena that let her know that her work was not in vain. Following a speech in Galveston, Texas, a woman pushed her way through the crowd.

"Miss Aguillard, may I speak to you?" she asked.

"Of course," said Vena.

"I just wanted to tell you," the woman began, "that I lived in Morgan City when you were a missionary there. I am ashamed to say that I was one of the ones who laughed at you from behind a closed door. I thought you were crazy then. But I want you to know that now I am a Christian, too."

Tears of gratitude filled Vena's eyes. Silently she thanked the Lord. "No matter how hard the work seems sometimes, Lord, you don't let any of it go to waste. You are working even when I can't see the results right away."

Camp Adventures

Vena watched the Oklahoma landscape flash by the train window. She wondered what lay ahead for her when she reached her destination. Vena prayed as she looked out of the window.

"Lord, you know how much I enjoy working in camps during the summer. Every camp is different. Each one gives me a chance to get to know some wonderful young people. And it is so good to be with other missionaries who also come to speak. But I really don't know what to expect at Camp Davis. I have been told that the Indian people are very serious. I've also heard that they don't talk much. I don't know how we will fellowship together. But that is in your hands, Lord. I know you can make a way," Vena prayed.

Vena looked out at four hundred beautiful brown faces at the first camp meeting. Four hundred pairs of dark eyes watched to see what Vena would do. Vena started with a story. She told what it was like to grow up in South Louisiana. Vena told them about the wonderful change that came into her life when she met Jesus at the age of eighteen. As she talked, the Indian people warmed up to Vena.

Before long, Vena was laughing, playing, praying, and worshiping with the Indian people at Camp Davis.

"Come play ball with us, Miss Vena," the young people called one afternoon.

"I've never played ball," Vena said. "Will you teach me?"

"Sure, we will teach you," the young people answered. They took Vena by the hands and pulled her with them to the baseball diamond. A baseball cap was plopped on Vena's head. The rest of the afternoon was full of laughter as Vena tried to learn to play ball. The Indian people had as much fun teaching as Vena did trying to learn.

"I don't know why anyone ever told me these delightful people

46

are reserved and quiet," thought Vena. "I have never had more fun than I have at this camp."

One summer, Vena went to a camp in Prescott, Arizona. She was to teach a missions book to the girls at the camp. Mrs. Brown, who was in charge of the camp, greeted Vena when she arrived.

"I'm afraid I have bad news for you," she said. "The girls say they won't take a study course. They said they came to camp to have fun, and study courses are boring. I am afraid you have come all this way for nothing."

Vena saw a large group of girls sitting under a tree. "I think I will go and visit with the girls, anyway," Vena said to Mrs. Brown.

"We know why you are here," the girls said when they saw Vena. "We've already told Mrs. Brown that study courses are boring. We won't come!"

"I agree with you," said Vena. "I've been to some pretty boring study courses myself. What I had in mind was a love story."

"A love story! That's different. We'll come to hear a love story," the girls said.

Vena told the story of Evangeline, written by Longfellow. The girls sat spellbound as they followed the adventures of Gabriel searching for his lost love, Evangeline.

"I have another story for you tomorrow," said Vena, when she finished the story. "But, of course, I realize you won't be coming to class."

The girls began to talk among themselves. Finally one of the girls spoke. "We have decided that we will come back tomorrow," she said.

The next day Vena told her own story of growing up in the French part of Louisiana. She told them about the missionary that visited her home when she was eighteen years old. She shared the feelings she had as she heard about Jesus for the first time. Soon, the girls were wrapped up in Vena's beautiful story. All week the girls continued to come to class.

"What did you do to those girls?" Mrs. Brown asked when the week ended. "They told me nothing would get them to take a study course."

"Oh, I tricked them," Vena chuckled. The girls never realized that the interesting stories they heard all week really were from the study course which they refused to take.

48

One year, Vena received an invitation to speak at a camp in Utah. "What a good experience that would be for my niece, Bonita. I think I'll ask her to come with me," Vena thought.

"Oh, Mena!" Bonita cried, using the pet name she called her aunt. "I would love to go with you." Bonita's active, teenage imagination went to work dreaming up romantic visions of traveling out West. She counted the days until the trip.

At last the time came for Vena and Bonita to travel to the mountains of Utah. When they arrived at the campgrounds, they could hardly believe their eyes.

"But, Mena!" Bonita said. "Where are the buildings? Where will we sleep? Where will we eat?"

"Welcome to our camp," greeted Brother Marks, director of the camp. "I'll show you to your tent. You can get settled until time for dinner. We will eat at six o'clock in the big tent. If you need any help, let me know."

Vena and Bonita looked at each other for a minute. Bonita's romantic dreams were fading fast! But Vena was not going to let the primitive conditions get the best of her. Soon, Vena and Bonita were busy trying to find places to put things in their tent.

"We can hang a rope across the tent to hang our clothes," said Vena. "And that little tree outside will be perfect for our cups, mirrors, toothbrushes and other small things."

Bonita didn't think anything about this place looked perfect. But since she was here, she would have to make the best of it. Soon Vena and Bonita had their tent arranged. The little tree by the tent looked like a Christmas tree when they finished hanging things from the branches.

Even though it was too early for dinner, Vena and Bonita decided to walk over to the big dining tent. When they arrived, Mrs. Marks was giving directions. The place bustled with activity. Everyone helped prepare the evening meal. Fresh vegetables and meat, kept cold in a nearby mountain stream, soon became a delicious meal for the five hundred campers.

After dinner, the campers sat on long benches in the open-air chapel for the evening worship service. Bonita was asked to play the organ for the service. She saw the little organ but no organ bench. In a few minutes, Brother Marks rolled an oil drum over for Bonita to sit on while she played.

"This certainly is going to be a different kind of experience," thought Bonita. "I wonder what will happen next."

Bonita didn't have to wait long for more adventure. One afternoon, she and Vena decided to rest during some free time. Bonita changed into a short nightgown to be more comfortable while she napped. A little while later, a windstorm hit the camp. Pop! Pop! Pop! One by one, the tent pegs came loose as blasts of wind hit the tent.

"Hold on to the center pole to keep the tent down. I'll go get help," Vena shouted to Bonita above the noise of the wind. She ran to find Brother Marks.

A few minutes later, Vena returned with Brother Marks and two other men. They could not keep from laughing when they saw Bonita. She was still hanging on to the tent pole with all of her strength. Her short nightgown billowed out like a parachute. Each gust of wind lifted Bonita's feet off the ground. The wind was so strong that it took all five people to keep the tent from blowing away.

"I can't believe all those men saw me standing there in my nightgown," thought Bonita. "I almost wish the wind had blown me away instead."

Animals also shared the grounds with the campers. One day when Vena and Bonita went into their tent to rest, they noticed a cow grazing nearby. While they napped, something suddenly frightened the cow. Wildly, the cow ran straight for Vena and Bonita's tent! Down came the tent as the cow plowed into it. Vena and Bonita scrambled out of the tent, as Brother Marks came running to remove the cow.

"I'm not sure who was more frightened—the cow, or you ladies," Brother Marks said to Vena and Bonita.

Finally the time came to pack and leave the Utah mountains.

"I will never forget this mountaintop experience," Vena said to Bonita. "We have had fun and adventure. But most of all this place reminds me of the wilderness of Sinai where the children of Israel camped after leaving Egypt. Brother Marks has been a wise leader, just as Moses was to the Israelites. Truly God has been with us during these days."

God Will Supply My Needs

"Will you pray for my church?"

"Please pray for my brother who is not a Christian."

"Remember my grandmother in prayer. She is ill."

People constantly asked Vena to pray for things that concerned them. She was happy to pray for the needs of others. Often she requested prayer from others, too. She asked people to pray about the meetings where she would speak. She urged her friends and family to pray for people who did not know Jesus as Savior. But there was one thing for which she never asked people to pray.

Vena never asked people to pray for her personal needs. She believed that God called her to serve him. She asked him for what she needed and trusted him to provide.

Early one spring, Vena left Louisiana to go to a meeting in Georgia. Since the weather was warm in Louisiana, she left her old coat at home. But when she stepped from the train in Georgia, she had a big surprise! The weather was icy cold. The people who met her at the train quickly borrowed a coat for Vena to wear.

While Vena was in Georgia, she received a call asking her to come to North Carolina to speak.

"What is the weather like there?" Vena asked her caller.

"We are still having winter here," was the reply.

"What will I do about a coat?" Vena wondered. "Well, I borrowed one here. Perhaps I can borrow one after I get to North Carolina."

Vena arrived in North Carolina and went straight to the first meeting where she would speak. At the close of the meeting, a woman pushed through the crowd.

"Do you know anyone who needs a coat?" the lady called to

Vena over the heads of the people in front of her.

"Yes, I do," replied Vena. "I'll tell you about it in a minute."

Later, the woman said, "I bought a new coat a few weeks ago. For some reason, I got one several sizes too small. Since I can't wear it, I want to give it to someone who can use it."

Vena told the woman about leaving her coat at home. The woman hurried to her house. Soon, she returned carrying a beautiful, warm, brown coat. When Vena tried the coat on, she found that it was a perfect fit.

"This is the nicest coat I've ever had," said Vena, thanking the woman.

Vena trusted the Lord to provide her with the material things she needed. But she also knew that as a woman traveling alone, she needed the Lord's protection. Because she spoke two or three times each day, Vena depended on the Lord to help her prepare messages. One time, the Lord gave Vena a message in a very unusual way.

After weeks of traveling to speaking engagements with no rest, Vena finally had a one-night break in her schedule.

"I am looking forward to a quiet evening," Vena said, returning to her hotel room after lunch. But as Vena got to her room, she began to have a strange desire to speak. In a minute, the words of a message began to come to Vena's mind.

"This is almost like listening to a tape recorder," Vena thought. "But this is not like any message I've ever spoken before."

Vena concentrated on the words forming in her thoughts. Soon, a whole message was fixed in her mind. Vena lay back on the bed, wondering about what had just happened.

"That was strange," she thought. "Why would I need a message? I have nowhere to speak."

Fifteen minutes later, the phone rang.

"Miss Aguillard," said a woman. "I hate to disturb you, but I have a problem. Four hundred women are at my church to hear a missionary speak. He just called to say he can't come. I didn't know what to do. Then someone told me you might be able to come and speak. I know this is short notice. You won't have time to prepare, but we would love to hear anything you want to say," the woman concluded.

"Oh, I am prepared," Vena said, chuckling. "I will be glad to come."

When Vena got off the phone, she began to talk to the Lord. "Lord, you knew that sharing with four hundred women would be more fun than loafing in a hotel room. Thank you for preparing me ahead of time so I was ready when the lady called."

Vena knew that no need was too large or too small for the Lord to care about. She found that to be true in her personal life. And as she spoke, she prayed that the Lord would use her to help meet the needs of missions in general. Time after time, this happened as she spoke to groups. Wealthy women often came weeping to the altar. They gave what they had to the cause of missions. Vena often left a meeting with a suitcase full of furs and jewelry to send to the Home Mission Board.

But not all of the people who gave were wealthy. Sometimes, even the very poor gave all of their savings. Vena felt sorry for one poor man who gave one hundred dollars which he had saved in a baking-powder can. She even considered returning the money to the man. Then she remembered a story in the Bible.

"Jesus saw the widow give all she had. He did not stop her from giving. I should not stop this man, either. The Lord will bless him for sharing with others," Vena said.

During the depression years, the 1930's, the whole country was struggling. No one had any money. People gave all they could to missions, but still the debts piled up. Finally, the Southern Baptist Convention asked people to give their gold jewelry to help pay off a large debt.

"I wish I could help in some way," Vena thought. "But I don't have anything of value to give." Suddenly, Vena remembered the gold necklace Teddy had given her so long ago. She still had it tucked away in a safe place.

"I can have a part after all," Vena said joyfully. She was so thankful to be able to help meet the needs of others.

A Place to Call Home

"Welcome home, Vena," said her sister, Euna.

"Mena's here! How long will you get to stay?" cried Euna's daughter, Bonita, running to meet her aunt.

"I will be here three days. I must leave on Monday," replied Vena.

"You never get to stay long enough," Bonita said.

"I know I am usually here for only a few days every two or three months," said Vena. "But I am so thankful that I have a family to come home to, even for short visits. I feel refreshed after being with you."

When Vena was not traveling, she stayed with her sister, Euna. The time at home was to be a time of rest. But to Vena, sharing Jesus with others was a way of life. That did not stop just because she stopped traveling. Vena knew God could use her wherever she was.

Euna's son, Benny, had a friend who lived next door to Euna's family. Benny and his friend, Chesley, often played together. As the boys grew older, they began to talk about their beliefs. Chesley was not a Christian. Chesley had arguments and questions that Benny could not answer.

"Chesley, next time my aunt is home, I'm going to take you to see her. She can answer your questions," Benny said.

The next time Vena came home for a visit, Benny took Chesley in to talk with his aunt. Chesley was full of questions. He had formed some strong beliefs on his own. He had trouble accepting so many things about Christianity. For more than a year, each time Vena was home, she and Chesley visited. They searched the Bible for answers to Chesley's questions. But still he had doubts.

"Lord, I am just about to give up on this one," Vena prayed. "I can't seem to find a way to help him understand about you."

Then one Sunday, as the family prepared to go to church, Chesley knocked on the door.

"May I go to church with you?" he asked.

"Of course you can go," Benny said, trying not to show his surprise.

Chesley listened closely to the preacher's words that morning. At the close of the service, Chesley made a profession of faith in Jesus Christ. Within a few weeks, other members of his family became Christians also.

One time when Vena came home for a short stay, Euna told her some news.

"Our friend in Chataignier is very ill. Can we go see him right now? I want you to talk to him about Jesus," Euna said.

Vena was very tired from her travels. "I think I should rest first," she said. "Then I will feel more like talking with him."

Vena tried to rest. But she could not get the man off her mind. Finally, Vena got up and found Euna.

"Let's go to Chataignier. I'll rest later. This is more important," Vena said.

As soon as Vena saw the man, she knew he could not live long. "I want to tell you about Jesus," Vena said to her friend. Vena told the man how he could be saved by believing in Jesus Christ. She read to him from the Bible.

"I believe what the Scriptures say. I want Jesus as my Savior," said the man in a weak voice.

Vena prayed with her friend, and he accepted Jesus as his Savior. Vena and Euna returned home. Just as they walked in the house, the telephone rang. Euna answered the phone and listened for a minute. Slowly, she replaced the receiver.

"Vena, we reached our friend just in time," Euna said. "He died just after we left his home."

"Thank you, Lord, for helping me know that I should go, even though I was tired. Thank you that we got to his home in time to tell him about you. Thank you that he is with you now, because he accepted you as his Savior," Vena prayed.

Finally, the time came when Vena had to make a decision about retiring from missions work. She had never thought about retirement before. She expected to be involved in missions work all of her life. But gradually she was forced to slow down. Constant traveling and speaking began to affect her health. Finally, she realized that she could no longer be an effective field missionary. Vena began to pray about what she should do next.

"Lord, I know you have a plan for me now. You have provided for me since I became your child. Show me where I am to live for the rest of my life," Vena prayed.

Vena went to stay with her sister, Euna. By this time, Bonita and Benny were married and had homes of their own. Vena knew she could stay with Euna until she knew what the Lord had in his plan for her. Soon the Lord made his plans clear. Bonita's husband, Robert Reeves, came to see Vena and Euna.

"Bonnye and I want both of you to make your home with us," he said. "We have plenty of room for you in our house. We want to provide for you and take care of you."

So Vena and Euna went to live with Bonnye and Robert. Vena thanked God for taking care of her.

"Lord, long ago I found a verse in my Bible. The verse says, 'In all thy ways acknowledge him, and he shall direct thy paths' (Proverbs 3:6). I know that you have directed my paths since I asked you to be my Savior. Thank you for directing my paths at this time in my life. Bonita and Robert have such a lovely Christian home. And Euna and I can be together. I feel so happy knowing that I can spend the rest of my life with my family," Vena prayed.

Many people who knew Vena Aguillard thought she gave up so much to follow the Lord. But Vena did not see things that way. She saw only the blessings given to her by the Lord. Looking back on her life, Vena saw the blessing of having her whole family trust Jesus as Savior. She recalled the many Christian friends she had. She thought about the joys of serving Jesus. Vena remembered the countless people who had accepted Jesus as she talked to them. She thought of the ways God had met her needs each day. Vena knew that she gained so much more than she gave up.

Vena said, "The way the Lord has blessed my life reminds me of something Jesus taught. He said that those who give up family or material possessions to follow the Lord will receive back a hundred

59

times over in this life. Then in the life to come, they will receive eternal life. I have received more than a hundred times over in blessings. And I can look forward to spending eternity in fellowship with my wonderful Lord."

Remember . . .

Vena Aguillard had many qualities that made her a great woman. The questions below will help you recall times when Vena demonstrated various qualities. You will also find questions to help you think about these same qualities in your life.

- Vena was *helpful*. What did she do to be helpful when she was a little girl? How did God use her helpful nature to start a church in Morgan City? Name something you have done recently to be helpful.
- Vena *got along well with others*. What did she do in Prescott, Arizona, to find a way to get along with the girls at summer camp? Have you ever had to make a special effort in order to get along with someone?
- Vena was *obedient*. How do you know that Vena was obedient as a little girl? Was she still obedient as a teenager? When was Vena obedient to God, even when it was hard? Have you ever obeyed when it was hard? What did you do?
- Vena was *courageous*. How did Vena show courage when everyone said it was impossible to reach the people of Abbeville for Jesus? Recall a time when you showed courage in a difficult situation.
- Vena was *dedicated to God*. How did Vena show her dedication to God, even though it meant losing friends? Have you ever had to make a decision to do right, even though it meant going against the crowd?
- Vena was a *witness for Jesus*. Who were the first people Vena told about Jesus after she became a Christian? Who were some people Vena witnessed to while she was at home for a rest? Think of some ways that you can be a witness for Jesus.

- Vena was a person who *prayed*. What experience at Acadia Baptist Academy helped her learn how the Lord works through prayer? Have you ever prayed for something special? How did God answer your prayer?
- Vena had a *sense of humor*. What funny thing happened to Vena while she was riding a troop train to a speaking engagement? Do you think Vena could have spoken under those circumstances if she did not have a sense of humor? Name a time when you have had to laugh at yourself when something funny happened.
- Vena had *faith in God*. What did she do to remind herself of God's promises? Name some ways God supplied Vena's needs. Name one way God has recently met a particular need for you.

About the Author

My name is Marsha Barrett. I live in Longview, Texas, with my husband and daughter. On Sundays, I teach boys and girls who are about the same age as you.

It is really exciting to me to see boys and girls begin to discover the joy of serving Jesus. That is why I am so glad that I could write this book about Vena Aguillard. I knew that boys and girls who read about her might understand more about what it means to give their lives to Jesus.

I pray for boys and girls who read this book. I pray that this book will help boys and girls like you want to serve Jesus. You might not be a missionary like Vena Aguillard. But if you tell Jesus that you give your life to him, he will begin to show you his special plan for you.